ART NOUVEAU TYPOGRAPHIC ORNAMENTS

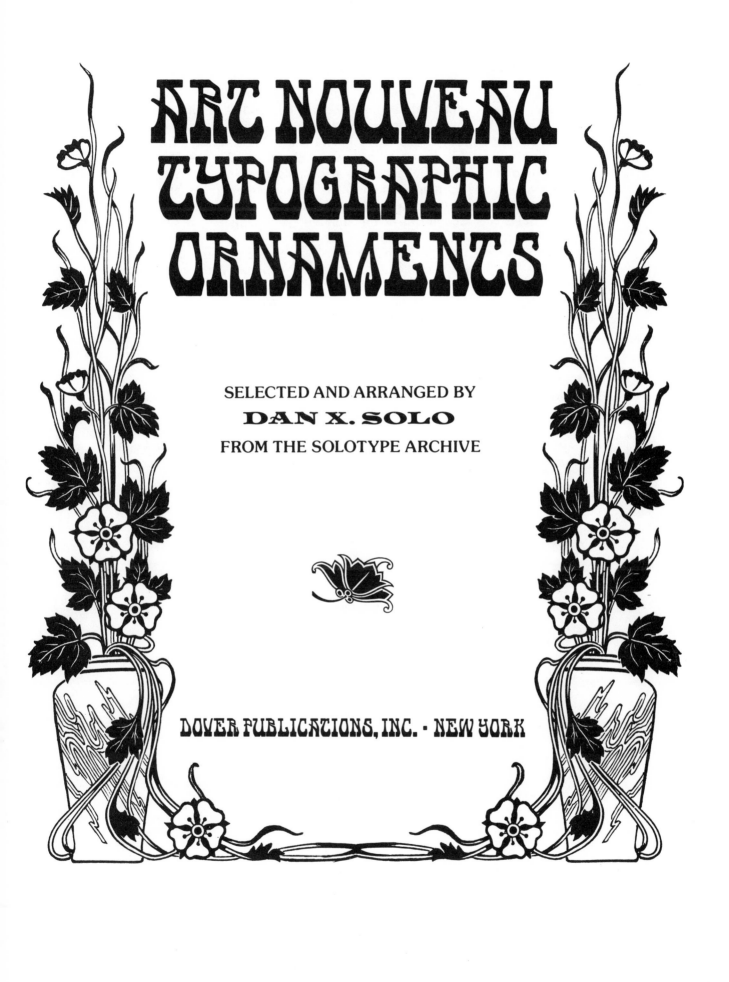

ART NOUVEAU TYPOGRAPHIC ORNAMENTS

SELECTED AND ARRANGED BY

DAN X. SOLO

FROM THE SOLOTYPE ARCHIVE

DOVER PUBLICATIONS, INC. • NEW YORK

PUBLISHER'S NOTE

Here is a treasury of authentic Art Nouveau typographic ornament selected from specimen catalogues of leading European and American type foundries in the Solotype Archive. Dan Solo's gleanings from these rare sources provide today's graphic designers with a wide variety of borders, spot illustrations, head- and tailpieces, dingbats, scrolls, wreaths, menu plates and more. This collection is especially rich in floral and plant ornaments, including many recognizable flowers, trees, fruits and vines. Animal motifs — butterflies, dragonflies, fishes, lions, peacocks, pheasants, snails and turtles–abound, as do fluid renderings of human figures, fabulous creatures and other, purely decorative elements.

Mirror images of many of these sharply printed designs are provided for maximal flexibility of application. To evoke sensuality or *fin-de-siècle* nostalgia, graphic artists often turn to the Art Nouveau style. What better source of harmonious ornament to complement a display setting of Bocklin, Metropolitan or Auriol? This book is the perfect companion to Solo's *Art Nouveau Display Alphabets: 100 Complete Fonts* (Dover 1976, 0-486-23386-3).

Much of the material published here originally appeared in late 19th-century and early 20th-century catalogues of the following printers and typesetters: Barnhart Bros. & Spindler (Chicago); H. Berthold (Berlin & Stuttgart); Deberny et Peignot (Paris); Joh. Enschedé & Sons (Haarlem); "Amsterdam"; Vanderborght (Brussels); E. J. Genzsch (Munich); Successors to Benjamin Krebs (Frankfurt); Keystone (Philadelphia); "Plantin" (Brussels); J. G. Schelter & Giesecke (Leipzig); Van Loey-Nouri (Brussels); and Wilhelm Woellmer (Berlin).

Copyright © 1982 by Dover Publications, Inc.
All rights reserved under Pan American and International Copyright Conventions.

Published in Canada by General Publishing Company, Ltd., 30 Lesmill Road, Don Mills, Toronto, Ontario.
Published in the United Kingdom by Constable and Company, Ltd.

Art Nouveau Typographic Ornaments is a new work, first published by Dover Publications, Inc., in 1982.

DOVER *Pictorial Archive* SERIES

Manufactured in the United States of America
Dover Publications, Inc.
31 East 2nd Street
Mineola, N.Y. 11501

Library of Congress Cataloging in Publication Data

Solo, Dan X.
Art Nouveau typographic ornaments.

Bibliography: p.
1. Type ornaments. 2. Decoration and ornament — Art nouveau. I. Title.
Z250.3.S65   1982   686.2'24   82-4577
ISBN 0-486-24366-4   AACR2

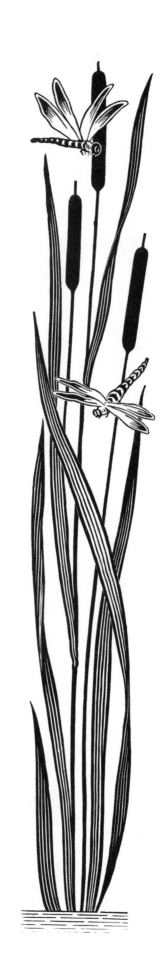

4

5

24

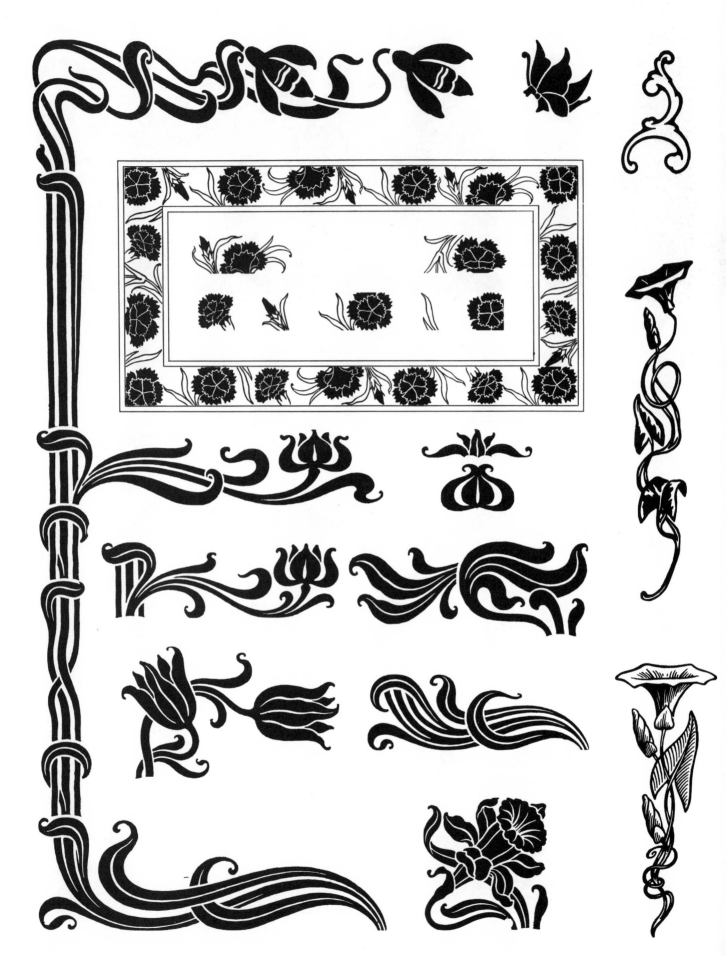

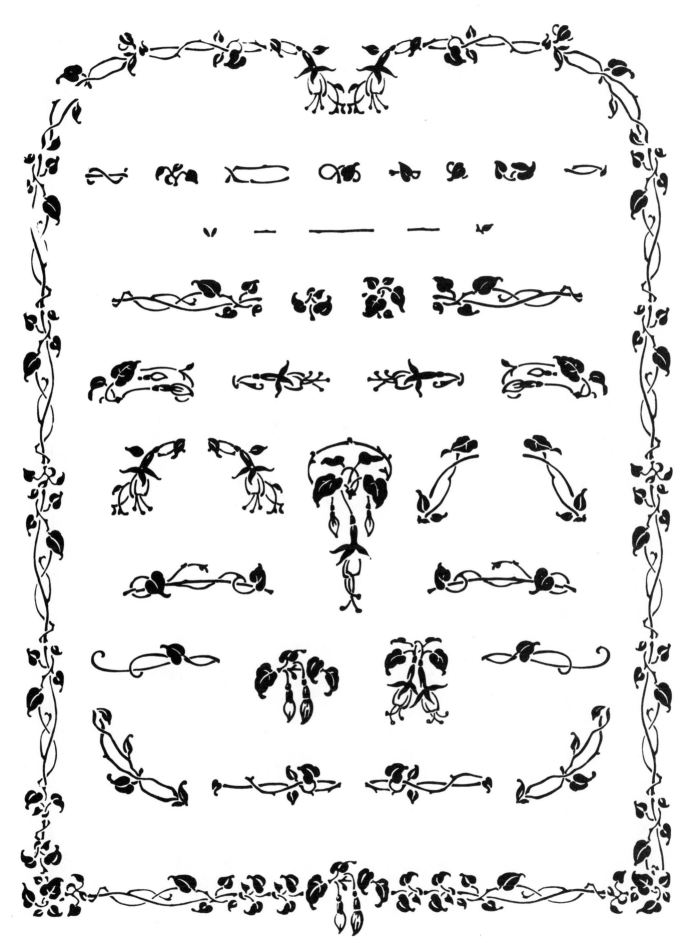

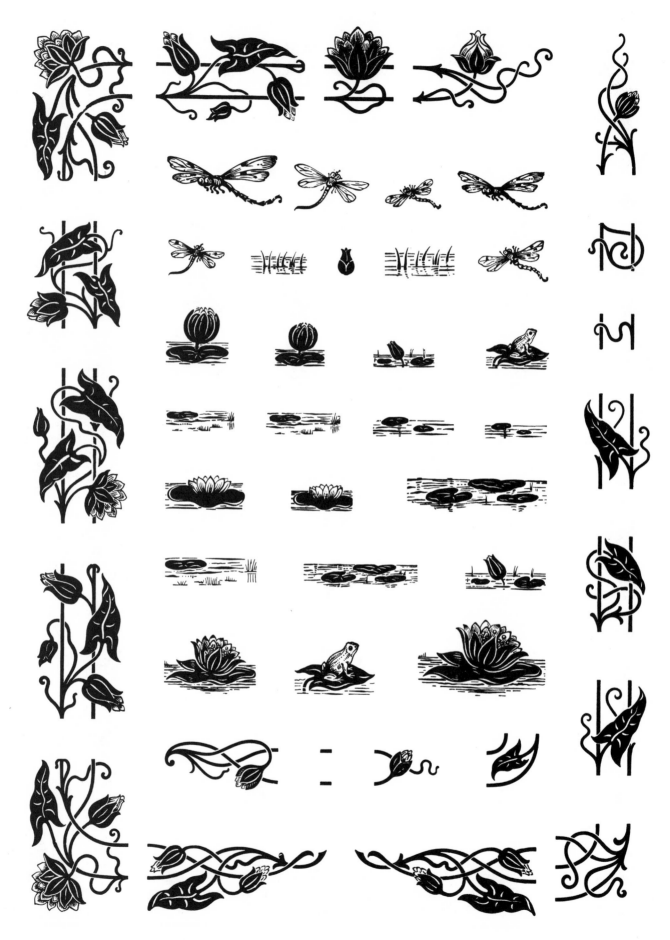

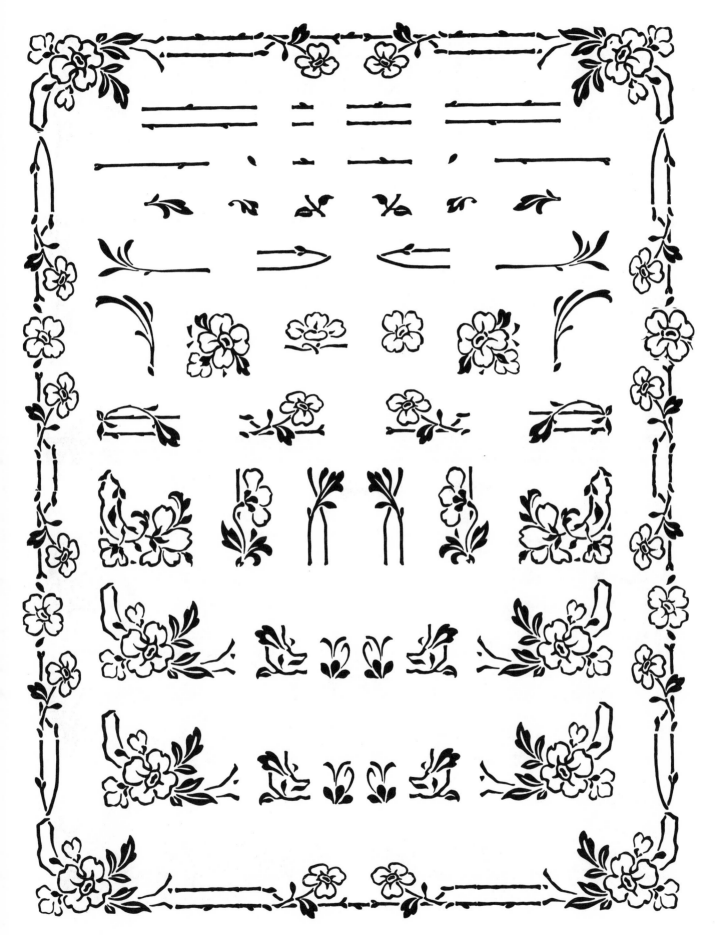

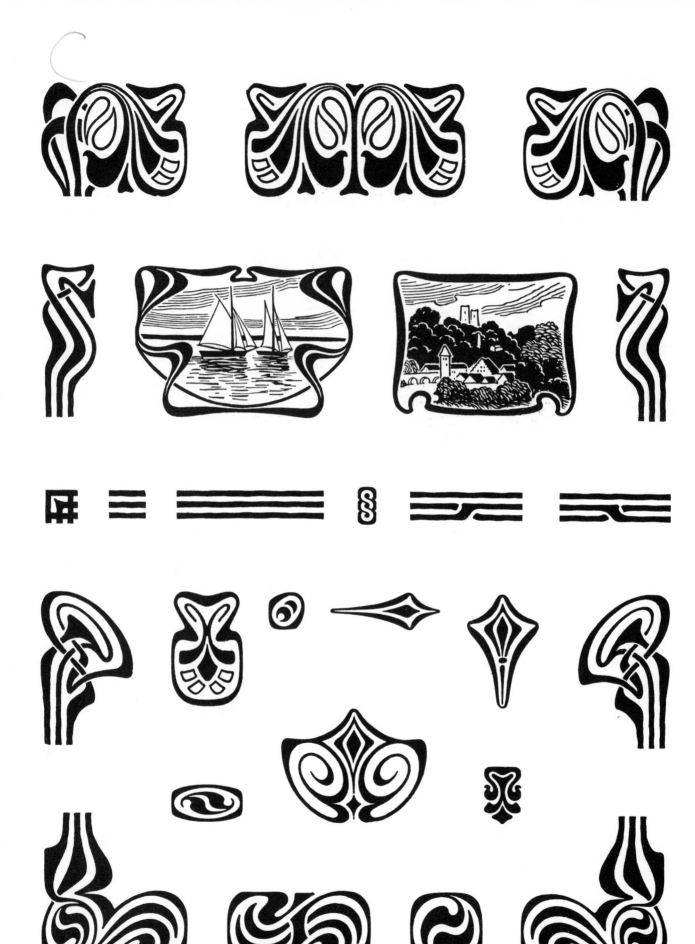

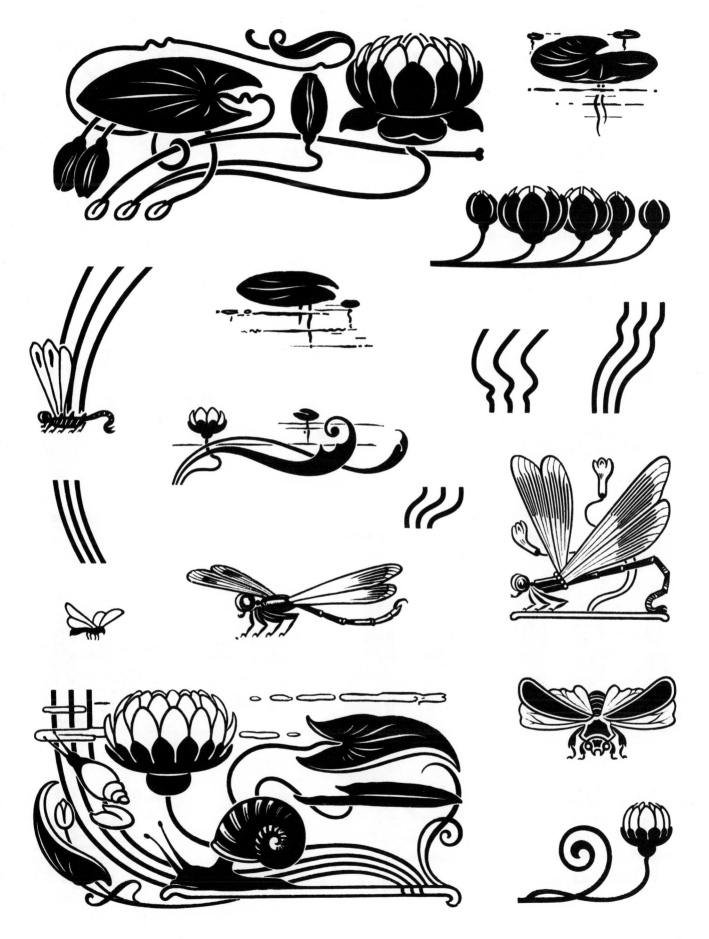

48

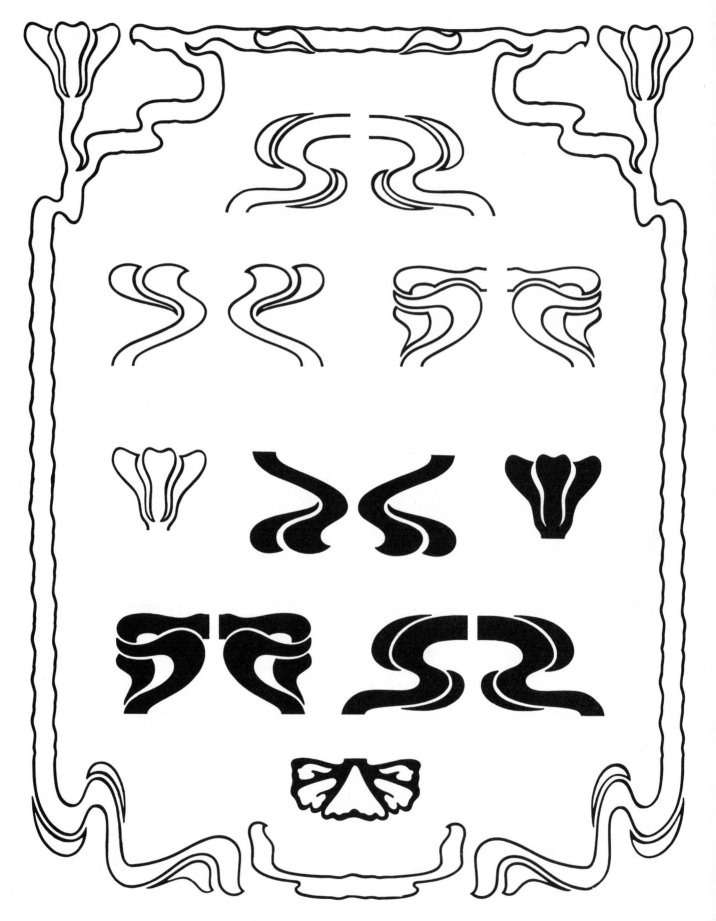

MENU

Menu

60

Memorandum

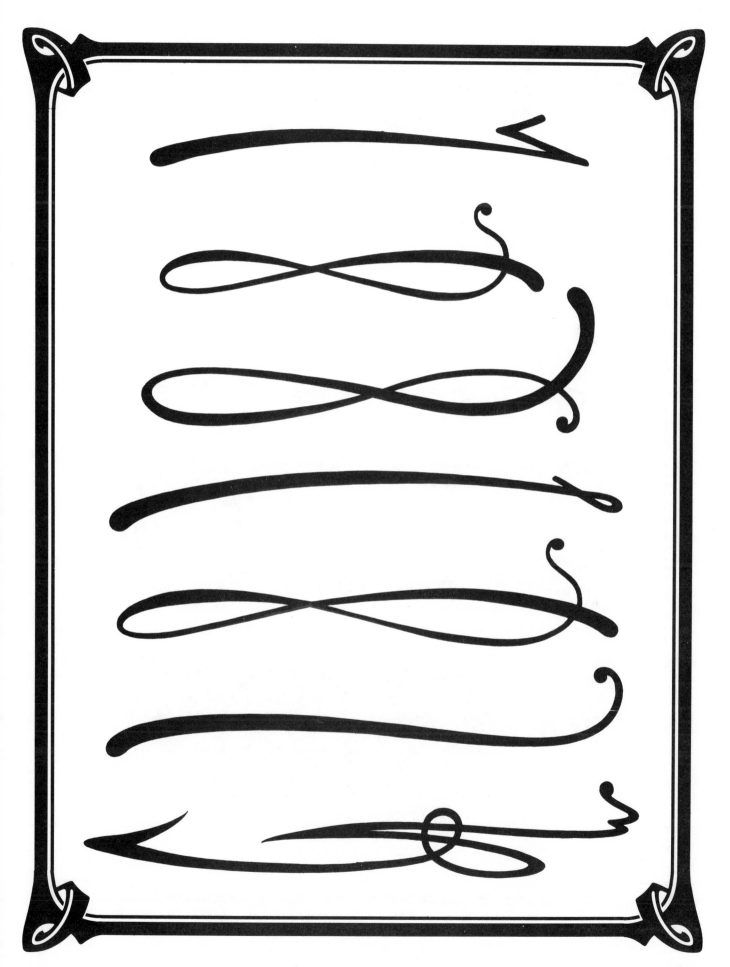

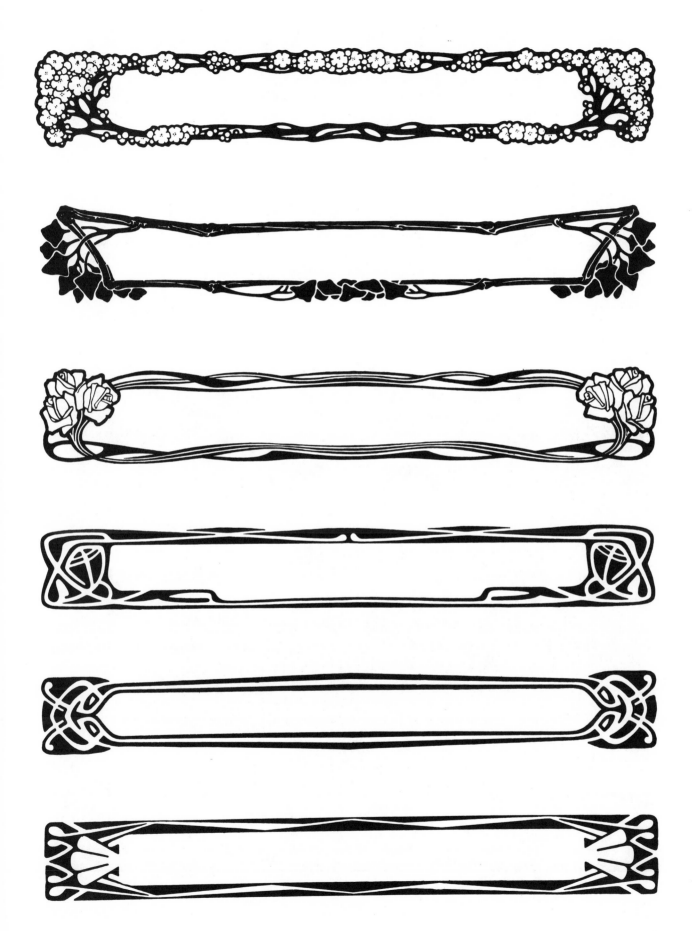

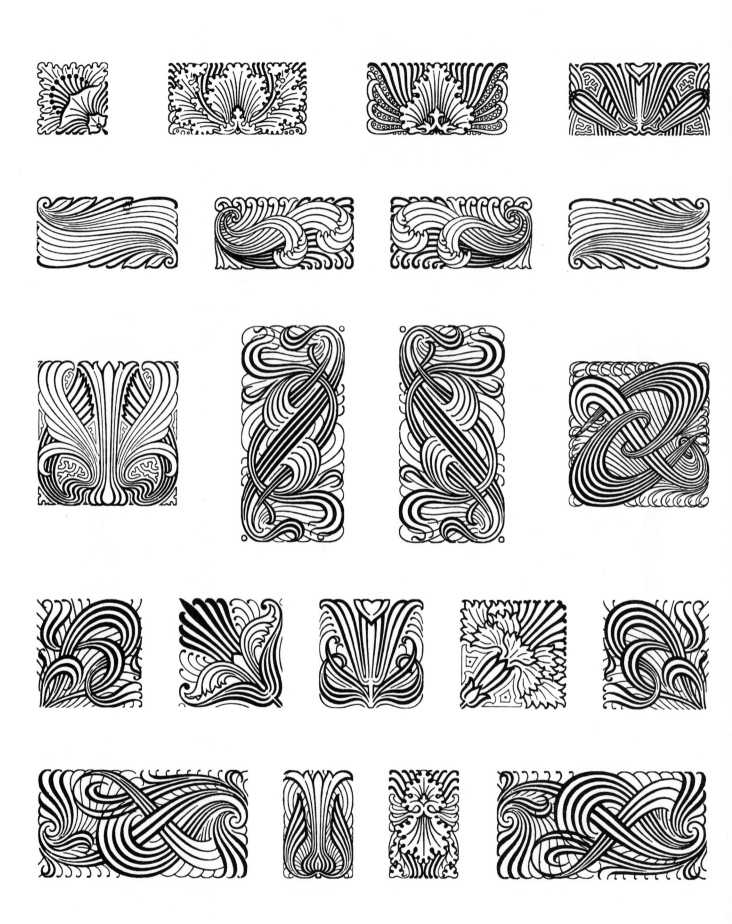

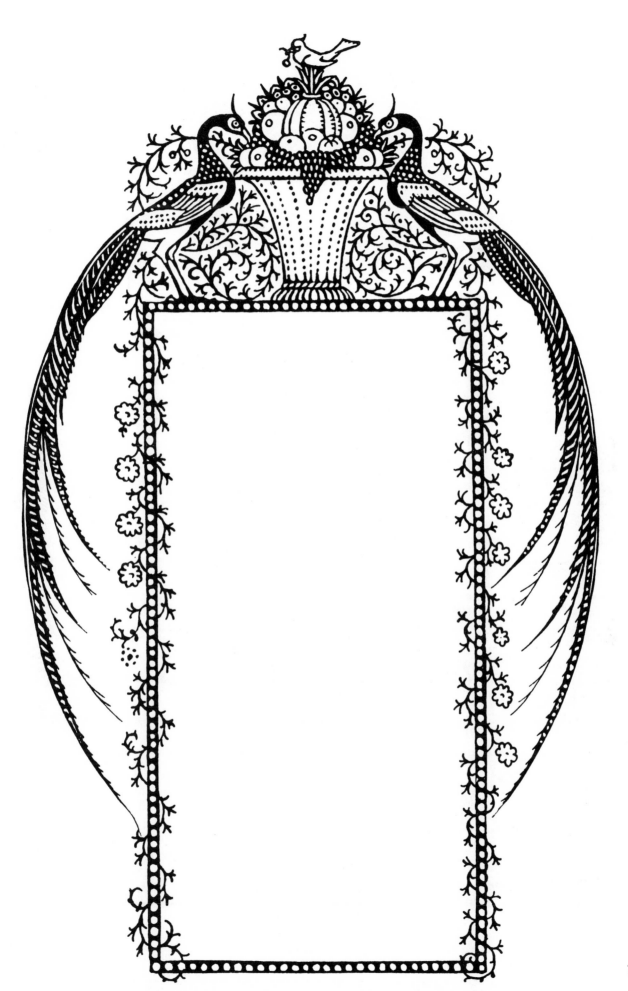

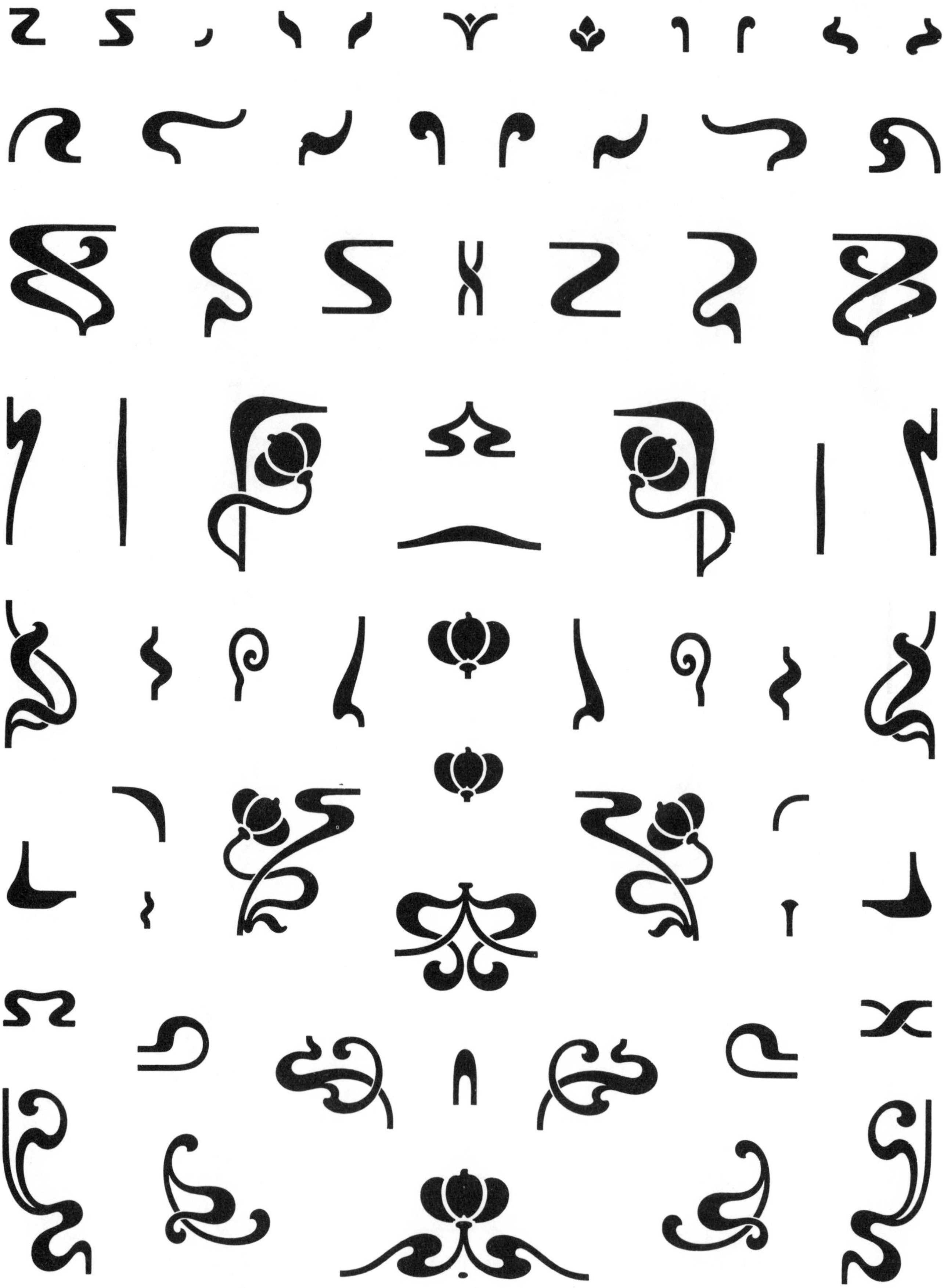

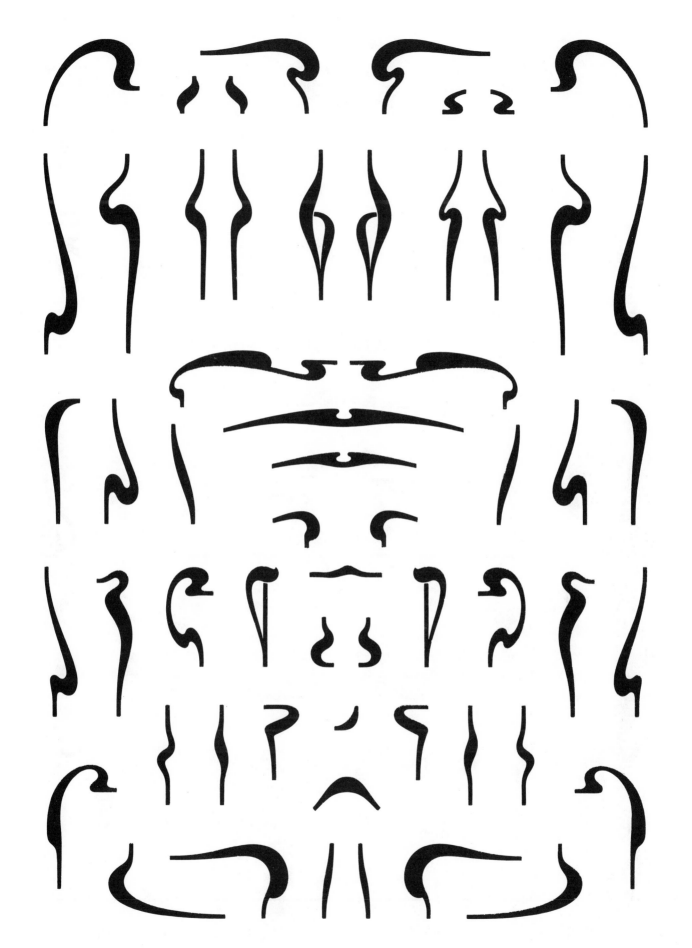

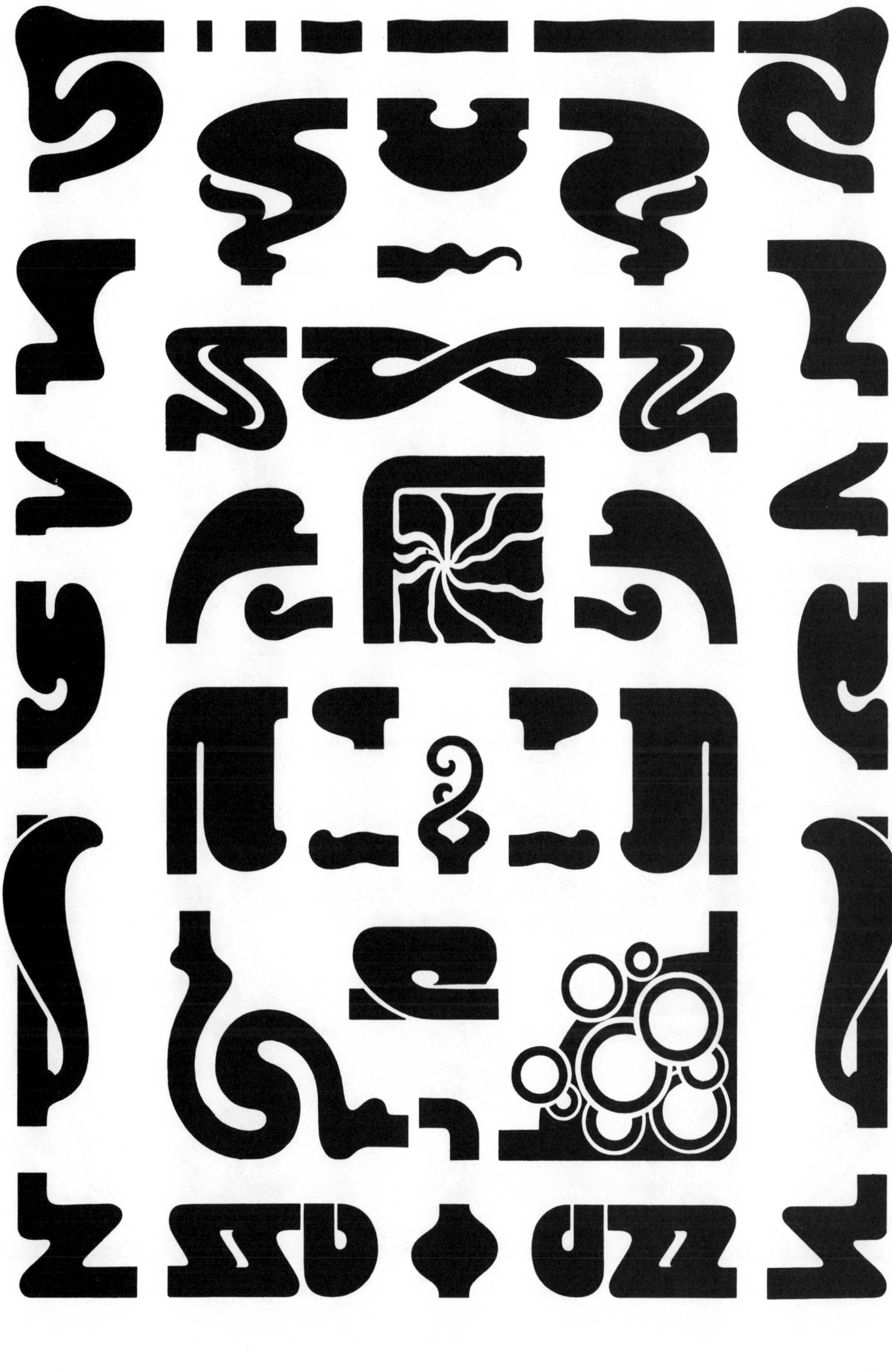

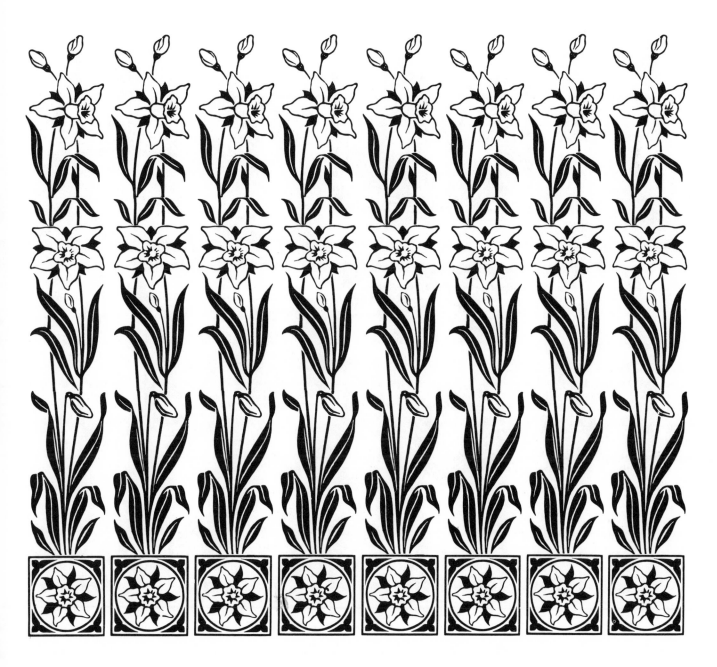

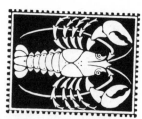

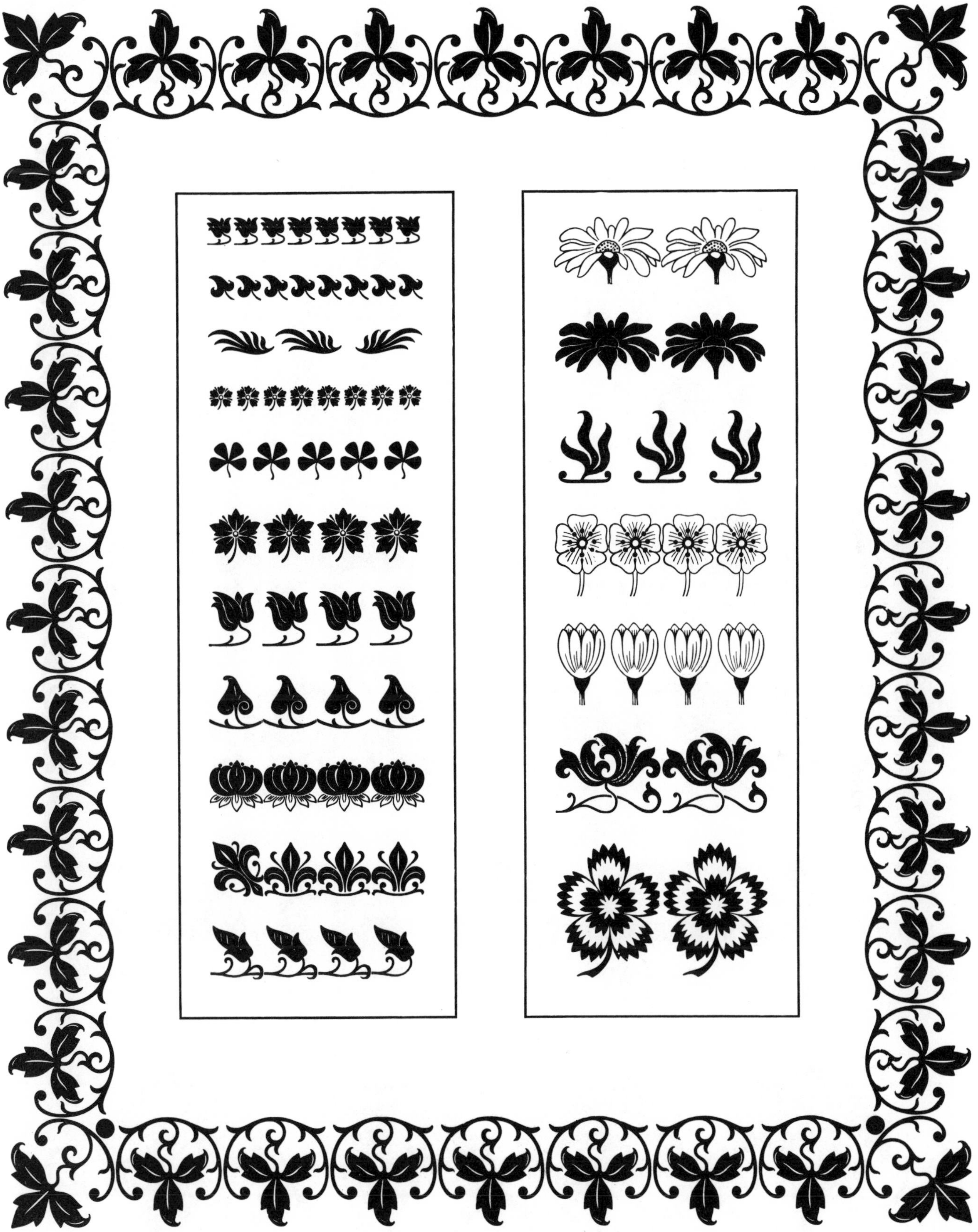

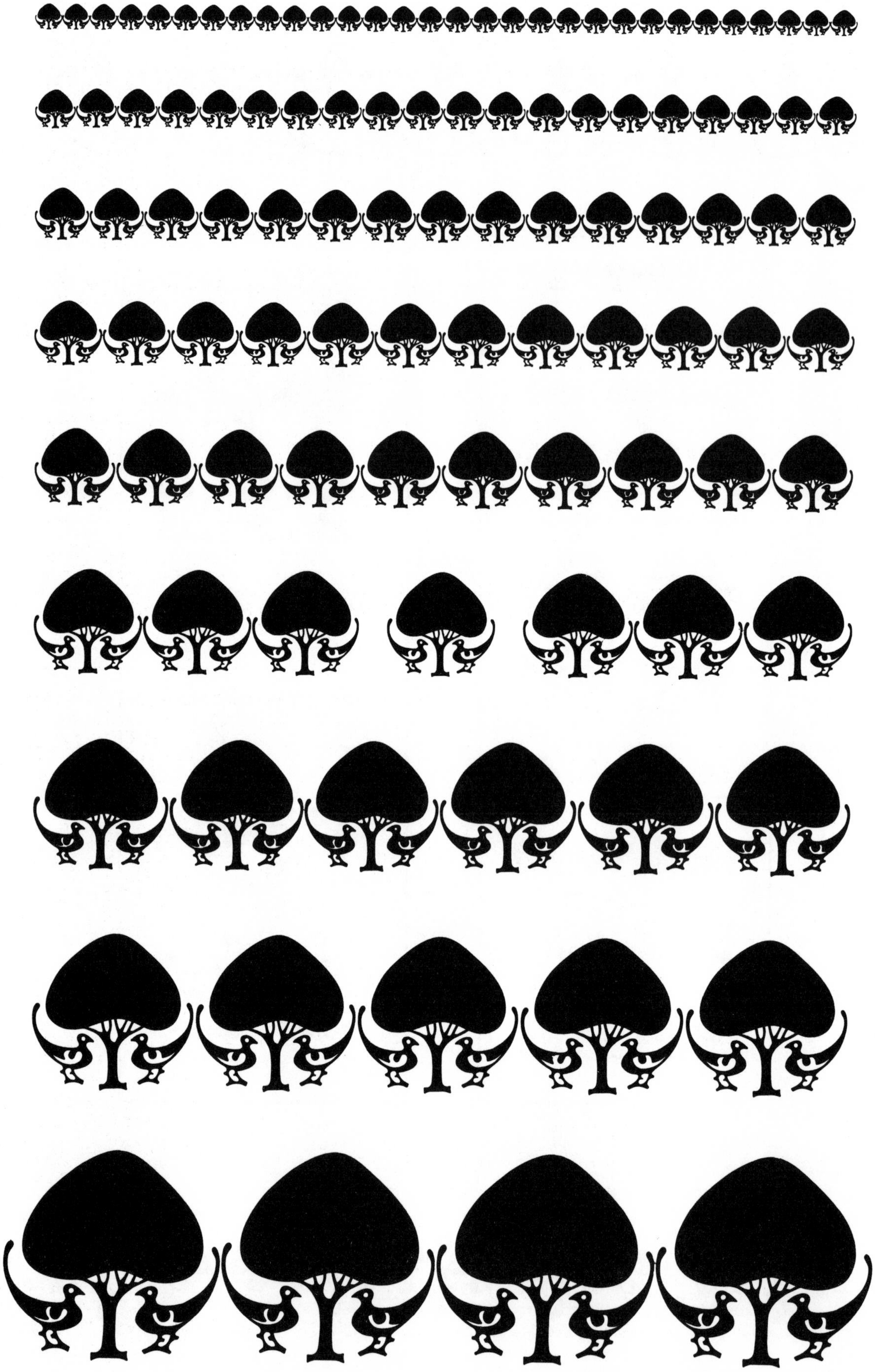

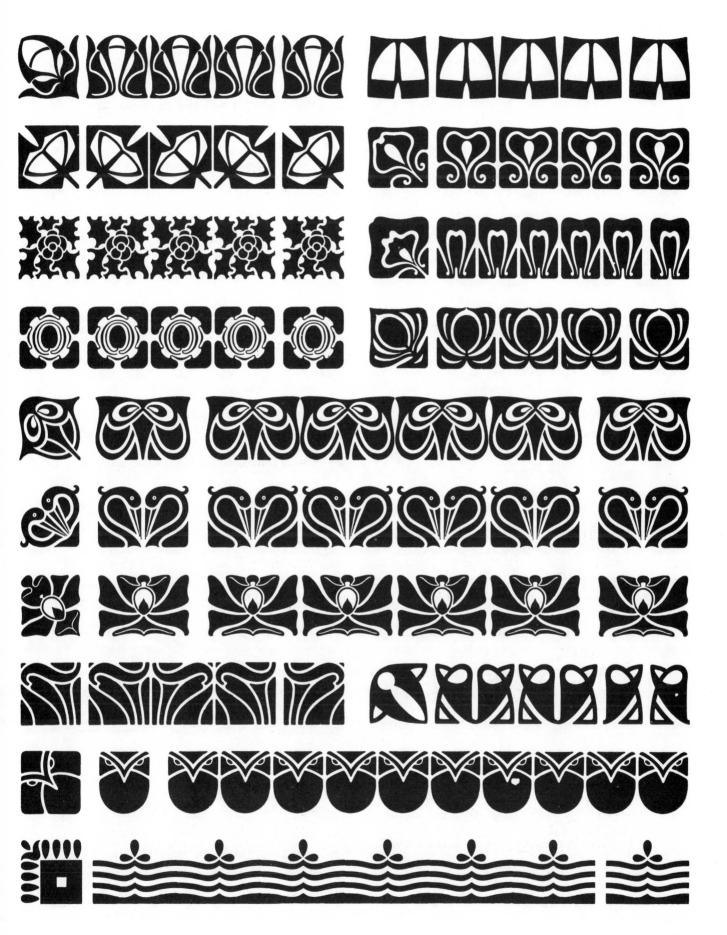

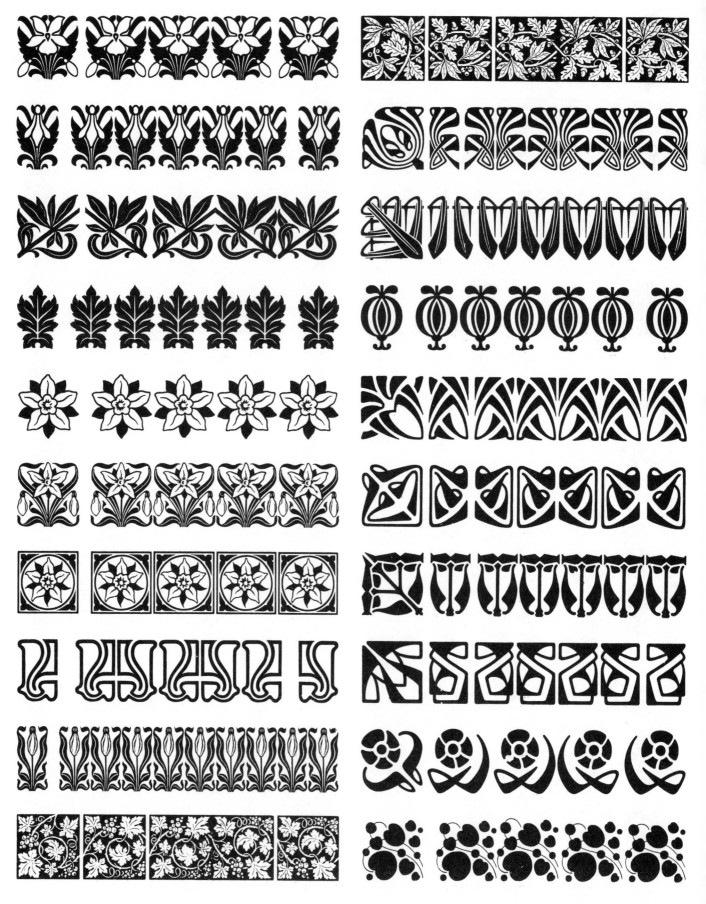

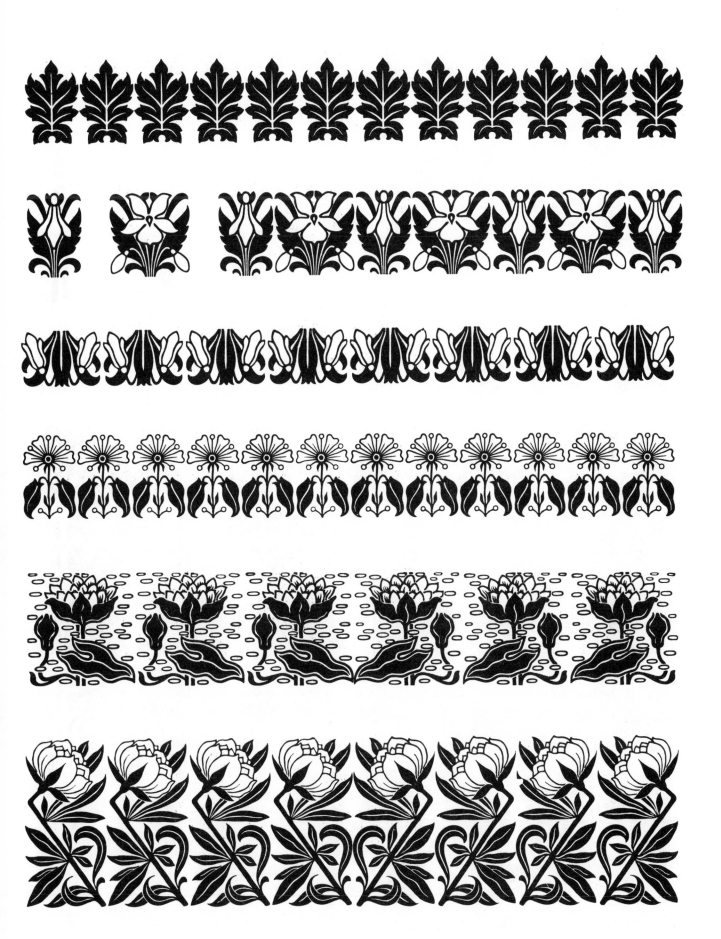